AaBbCcDdEeFfGgHh

The ABCs of
Continents

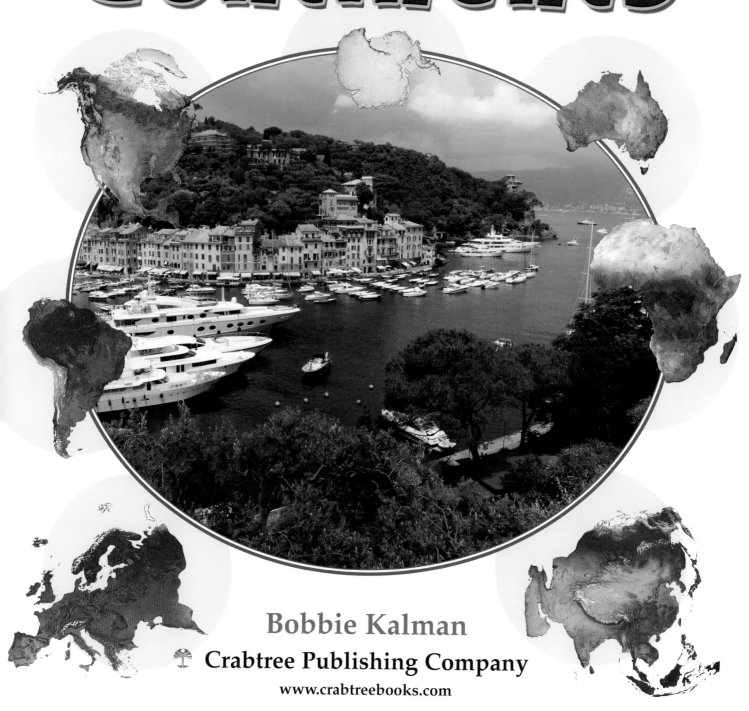

Bobbie Kalman

🌿 **Crabtree Publishing Company**

www.crabtreebooks.com

A a B b C c D d E e F f G g H h

The ABCs of the Natural World

Created by Bobbie Kalman

Dedicated by Crystal Sikkens
To Matt and Lisa Snippe and their new baby boy, Carson Anthony

Author and Editor-in-Chief
Bobbie Kalman

Editor
Kathy Middleton

Proofreader
Crystal Sikkens

Photo research
Bobbie Kalman
Crystal Sikkens

Design
Bobbie Kalman
Katherine Berti
Samantha Crabtree (cover)

Production coordinator
Katherine Berti

Illustrations
Barbara Bedell: pages 5 (coral, sea anemone, and pink fish),
14 (light blue fish, green fish, striped fish, coral, and crab),
15 (pink fish, coral-left and sea anemone-left)
Katherine Berti: pages 4 (map), 5 (map and dark blue fish),
6, 8, 12, 13, 14 (dark blue fish), 18
Robert MacGregor: pages 1 (maps), 15 (top right)
Vanessa Parson-Robbs: page 14 (purple fish)
Bonna Rouse: page 15 (sea anemone-right and green coral-right)
Margaret Amy Salter: pages 5 (yellow fish and crab),
14 (yellow fish), 15 (yellow fish)
Tiffany Wybouw: pages 5 (dolphin)

Photographs
© Dreamstime.com: pages 7 (bottom left), 21 (girl),
22 (except amethyst)
© Shutterstock.com: cover, pages 1 (middle), 3, 4 (top),
6, 7 (background and top right), 8, 9, 10, 11, 12, 13, 14,
15 (except top right), 16, 17, 18, 19, 20, 21 (boys),
22 (amethyst), 23, 24, 25, 26, 27, 28, 29 (except top right),
30, 31
Other images by Digital Stock

Library and Archives Canada Cataloguing in Publication

Kalman, Bobbie, 1947-
    The ABCs of continents / Bobbie Kalman.

(The ABCs of the natural world)
Includes index.
ISBN 978-0-7787-3414-7 (bound).--ISBN 978-0-7787-3434-5 (pbk.)

    1. Continents--Juvenile literature. 2. English
language--Alphabet--Juvenile literature. I. Title.
II. Series: Kalman, Bobbie, 1947- . ABCs of the natural world.

G133.K34 2009   j910.914'1   C2008-907878-0

Library of Congress Cataloging-in-Publication Data

Kalman, Bobbie.
    The ABCs of continents / Bobbie Kalman.
        p. cm. -- (The ABCs of the natural world)
    Includes index.
    ISBN 978-0-7787-3434-5 (pbk. : alk. paper) -- ISBN 978-0-7787-3414-7
(reinforced library binding : alk. paper)
    1. Continents--Juvenile literature. 2. Alphabet books--Juvenile
literature. I. Title. II. Series.

G133.K25 2009
910.914'1--dc22

2008052352

Crabtree Publishing Company

www.crabtreebooks.com   1-800-387-7650

Published in Canada
Crabtree Publishing
616 Welland Ave.
St. Catharines, Ontario
L2M 5V6

Published in the United States
Crabtree Publishing
PMB16A
350 Fifth Ave., Suite 3308
New York, NY 10118

Published in the United Kingdom
Crabtree Publishing
White Cross Mills
High Town, Lancaster
LA1 4XS

Published in Australia
Crabtree Publishing
386 Mt. Alexander Rd.
Ascot Vale (Melbourne)
VIC 3032

Contents

The "A" continents

EARTH

Earth has huge land areas called **continents**. There are seven continents. Find them on the map below. The names of six of the seven continents start with the letter A. America is broken into two continents. What are they? Which continent starts with the letter E?

The seven continents are Asia, Africa, North America, South America, Antarctica, Europe, and Australia and Oceania.

NORTH AMERICA

ATLANTIC OCEAN

PACIFIC OCEAN

SOUTH AMERICA

Asia is the biggest continent. Australia and Oceania make up the smallest continent.

4

Bb Bb Bb Bb Bb Bb Bb Bb

Big bodies of water

Oceans are the biggest bodies of water on Earth. They surround most of the continents. There are five oceans on Earth. They are the Pacific Ocean, Atlantic Ocean, Indian Ocean, Southern Ocean, and Arctic Ocean. Which is the biggest ocean? Which is the smallest? Look at the map and take a guess. The answers are below.

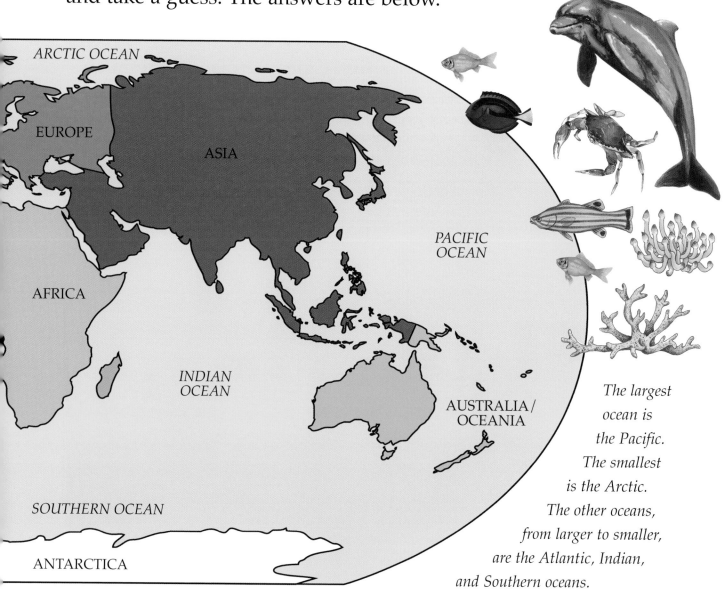

ARCTIC OCEAN

EUROPE

ASIA

AFRICA

PACIFIC OCEAN

INDIAN OCEAN

AUSTRALIA/ OCEANIA

SOUTHERN OCEAN

ANTARCTICA

The largest ocean is the Pacific. The smallest is the Arctic. The other oceans, from larger to smaller, are the Atlantic, Indian, and Southern oceans.

5

Cc Cc Cc Cc Cc Cc Cc Cc Cc

Countries and cities

Countries are parts of continents. A country is an area of land with **borders** and a **government**. A border is where one country ends and another begins. A government makes decisions for people who live in a country. Most countries have **cities**. Cities are places with many buildings and people. Millions of people live and work in big cities.

Canada is a country whose name starts with the letter C. Canada is the largest country in North America and the second-largest country in the world. This Canadian city is Calgary. It is Canada's fourth-largest city. Calgary is in the province of Alberta. Which is the second-largest country in North America? It is Canada's neighbor, the United States!

Dd Dd Dd Dd Dd Dd Dd Dd

Dry deserts

There are **deserts** on every continent on Earth. Deserts are dry places that can be hot or cold. Very little **precipitation** falls in deserts. Precipitation is rain or snow. The biggest hot desert on Earth is the Sahara Desert. It is in Africa. Near the North Pole, there is a huge area of frozen desert called the **tundra**. Much of northern Canada and Alaska are covered by tundra.

These polar bears live on the frozen tundra in the Arctic. Part of the Arctic is in North America. Which ocean is part of the Arctic?

cacti

The coyote in the picture above lives in the hot Sonoran Desert in the United States. Plants called cacti grow in the Sonoran Desert.

*These people are riding camels in the Sahara Desert. Much of the Sahara Desert is covered with sand **dunes**. Dunes are formed when the wind blows sand into mounds and ridges.*

dunes

Europe

France's tallest and most famous building is the Eiffel Tower. People from all over the world come to Paris to climb this amazing structure.

Europe is a continent with 46 countries. It is joined to the continent of Asia. Russia is a country that is in both Europe and Asia. Some parts of Europe have four seasons: winter, spring, summer, and fall. Some parts of Europe are warm all year long. There are also parts of Europe that are cold for most of the year. There are many big, old, beautiful cities in Europe, such as Paris, Vienna, London, Rome, and Athens.

Europe's cities have beautiful buildings and famous works of art. This building in Rome, Italy, has a fountain. People throw coins into the fountain, hoping that their wishes will come true.

F f F f F f F f F f F f F f F f F f F f F f F f

Four directions

The four main directions on Earth are north, south, east, and west. The North Pole is at the top of Earth. The South Pole is at the bottom of Earth. The weather at both poles is cold all year long. At the center of Earth is the **equator**. The weather is always warm there. The equator divides Earth into two equal parts: the Northern Hemisphere and the Southern Hemisphere.

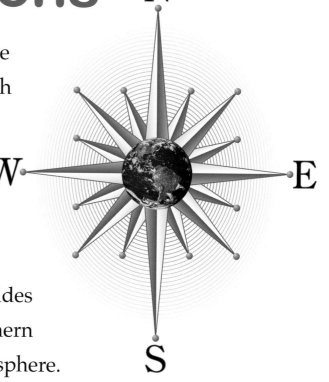

NORTH POLE

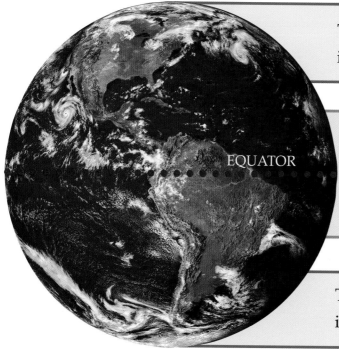

EQUATOR

SOUTH POLE

The Northern Hemisphere is above the equator.

The equator is an imaginary line around the center of Earth. Earth is covered mainly by oceans there.

The Southern Hemisphere is below the equator.

Grasslands on Earth

Grasslands grow all over the world. They are huge areas of grassy land with a few trees. In North America, grasslands are called **plains** or **prairies**. In South America, grasslands are called **pampas**. Some grasslands in Africa are called **savannas**.

*These bison live on the prairies in the middle part of North America. They **graze**, or feed on grasses.*

These guanacos live on a pampa in South America.

This giraffe lives on a savanna in Africa. The weather is hot and very dry during most of the year. Small trees and bushes grow on savannas.

H h H h H h H h H h H h H h

Habitats

Grasslands and deserts are two kinds of **habitats**. Habitats are natural places where animals live. Every continent has habitats. **Forests** are other kinds of habitats. Forests are areas with many trees. There are water habitats, too. Oceans, lakes, rivers, and **wetlands** are home to many animals.

These baby owls live in a forest habitat.

This young alligator lives in a wetland habitat. Wetlands are areas of land that are covered with water. Some wetlands are covered with water for most of the year. Other wetlands are covered with water for only part of the year. This wetland is in Everglades National Park in Florida.

I i I i I i I i I i I i I i I i I i I i I i I i

Iceland is an island

ICELAND

REYKJAVIK

EUROPE

Islands are land areas with water all around them. Iceland is a big island country that is part of Europe. Its capital city is Reykjavik. Iceland sits on top of **volcanoes** that are under the ocean. Iceland also has about 130 volcanic mountains on its land. Most people in Iceland speak Icelandic, English, and Danish.

These horses are grazing on a field in Iceland. There is a volcano behind them. Volcanoes that form on land can become tall mountains. Learn more about volcanoes on page 29.

Japan is in Asia

The country of Japan is made up of more than 3,000 islands in East Asia. This group of islands, or **archipelago**, is in the Pacific Ocean. The biggest island is called Honshu. Tokyo, Japan's capital city, is on this island. Japan is a mountainous country, and many of its mountains are volcanoes. Japan's name in Japanese is *Nippon*. *Nippon* means "land of the rising sun" because the sun rises in the east, where Japan is.

TOKYO

JAPAN

Tokyo is Japan's biggest city. It has beautiful parks.

13

Kingdoms of coral

Amazing **coral reefs** are among the wonders of the natural world because they are formed by tiny animals called **coral polyps**. When coral polyps die, their skeletons pile up and create reefs. Coral reefs form in calm, warm, shallow, clear oceans, where there is plenty of sunlight.

coral polyps

Great Barrier Reef

The biggest coral reef on Earth is the Great Barrier Reef. This huge reef is in the Coral Sea along the northeast coast of Australia. The reef is not one reef. It is made up of more than 3,000 separate reefs and 900 islands.

The yellow area on the map above is the Great Barrier Reef.

Many kinds of fish and other ocean animals live in coral reefs. This big fish is a reef shark.

L l L l L l L l L l L l L l L l L l L l

Landforms on Earth

The continents are Earth's biggest **landforms**. Landforms are the different shapes of land on Earth. In some places, the land is flat. In other places, the land is tall and steep. There are many kinds of landforms on each continent. Islands are one kind of landform. **Caves**, **canyons**, and **coasts** are also landforms.

Caves are landforms under the ground. They are hollow areas. Some look like big rooms.

Canyons are deep areas of land. Many canyons have rivers running through them.

Coasts are landforms where oceans meet land. The pictures above show different coastal landforms.

M m M m M m M m M m M m
Mountain landforms

Every continent on Earth has mountains. Mountains are big, tall, landforms of rocky land that rise high above the ground. Hills are small mountains with gently sloping sides. The highest mountain in the world is Mount Everest. It is in Asia. **Valleys** are flat landforms between mountains.

Mount Everest

Mount Everest is part of the Himalayan **mountain range**. *A mountain range is a group of mountains that forms a line.*

mountain

hill

valley

17

N n N n N n N n N n N n N n N n N n

North of the equator

GREENLAND

CANADA

UNITED
STATES

BAHAMAS

MEXICO

JAMAICA

Most of the land on Earth is north of the equator. North America, Europe, Asia, more than half of Africa, and parts of South America are north of the equator. North America is made up of 24 countries. The biggest four are Canada, the United States, Mexico, and Greenland. Some countries, such as the Bahamas and Jamaica, are islands.

The lands that are near the North Pole are called the Arctic. The winters are cold and snowy there. The Arctic is part of nine countries on three continents: Asia, Europe, and North America. The Arctic Ocean touches these continents.

N n N n N n N n N n N n N n N n

Russia is the largest country in Asia and in the world! It is so big that Moscow, its capital city, is in another continent. It is in Europe.

China is also part of the continent of Asia. It is one of the biggest countries on Earth. China's population is over 1.3 billion. More than one-sixth of the people on Earth live in China!

The Nile River is the longest river in the world. It is in the continent of Africa. This part of the Nile is flowing through Cairo, Egypt, which is north of the equator.

19

Oceania

Australia, and the thousands of islands that are near it, make up the continent of Australia and Oceania. The name Oceania was taken from the Pacific Ocean, where its islands are located. The country of New Zealand is part of Oceania. It is made up of North Island, South Island, and many smaller islands.

*Wellington is New Zealand's capital city. It is a big city. Many of the smaller islands in Oceania do not have cities. Some are **uninhabited**, which means that no people live on them.*

Pp Pp Pp Pp Pp Pp Pp Pp Pp Pp Pp Pp

People on Earth

There are almost 7 billion people on Earth! People live on every continent. More than half of them live in Asia. Africa has the second-largest **population**. Population is the number of people who live in one place. Fewer than 1,000 people live on the continent of Antarctica.

The country with the most people on Earth is China. India has the second-largest population. Both countries are on the continent of Asia.

What is culture?

People have different **cultures**. Culture is the way people live. It is the clothes they wear, the foods they eat, the languages they speak, and the ways they work and have fun.

This boy lives on his parents' ranch in Australia. He helps take care of the horses.

This girl lives in India. She is wearing a beautiful Indian dress.

Quartz is a mineral

This rock is an amethyst. It is a type of quartz.

Quartz is a **mineral**. A mineral is a non-living natural thing that forms in the Earth from heat and **pressure**. Our bodies need certain minerals. Without them, we could not stay alive for more than a few days! Quartz is the most common kind of mineral found on Earth. We cannot eat quartz, but it is used to run watches, television sets, telephones, computers, and many other important things.

*This rock is made of limestone. Quartz can be found in the cracks of limestone. This **rock formation** is in New Zealand. Learn about rock formations on page 23.*

R r R r R r R r R r R r R r R r R r

Rock formations

Earth's **crust** is the top layer of Earth. It is made of rock. Much of Earth is covered by plants and water, but you can see the rocky crust on Earth's mountains and rock formations. Rock formations are rocks with unusual shapes. The rock below is called Elephant Rock. It is made of a rock called sandstone.

These rock formations are called hoodoos.

S s S s S s S s S s S s S s S s S s S s S s

Southern continents

This guanaco is standing in front of the Andes, Earth's longest mountain range.

There are four continents south of the equator. They are South America, Antarctica, Australia and Oceania, and part of Africa. South America has **rain forests**, the longest mountain range, and the Amazon River, which is the second-longest river on Earth. The southern parts of South America are cold. They are near the continent of Antarctica.

Antarctica

Antarctica is the most southern place on Earth. It surrounds the South Pole. The land is covered with ice and snow. In some places, the Southern Ocean freezes into huge sheets of ice. In winter, there is no sunlight. In summer, the sun shines during the day and night. Penguins and seals live in Antarctica. Very few people live there.

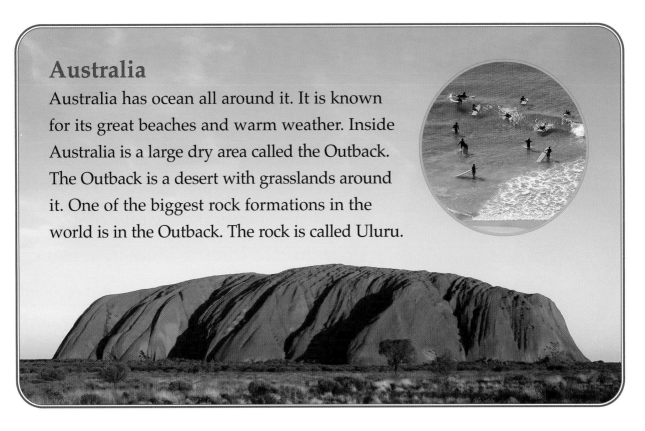

Australia

Australia has ocean all around it. It is known for its great beaches and warm weather. Inside Australia is a large dry area called the Outback. The Outback is a desert with grasslands around it. One of the biggest rock formations in the world is in the Outback. The rock is called Uluru.

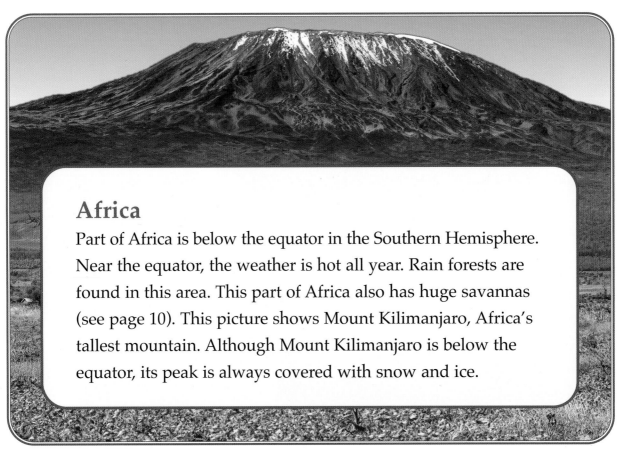

Africa

Part of Africa is below the equator in the Southern Hemisphere. Near the equator, the weather is hot all year. Rain forests are found in this area. This part of Africa also has huge savannas (see page 10). This picture shows Mount Kilimanjaro, Africa's tallest mountain. Although Mount Kilimanjaro is below the equator, its peak is always covered with snow and ice.

Tropical rain forests

Rain forests that are hot all year are called **tropical** rain forests. Tropical rain forests are in areas near the equator. They get rain nearly every day! Many plants grow in rain forests. More than half of all the world's plant and animal **species** live in tropical rain forests. Almost half of Earth's **oxygen** comes from rain forests. Oxygen is made by plants. It is the part of air that people and animals need to breathe.

Many kinds of tree frogs live in tropical rain forests.

This three-toed sloth lives in a tropical rain forest near the Atlantic Ocean in South America.

Orangutans are apes.
This orangutan lives
in a rain forest on an
island called Borneo.
Borneo is right at the
equator. It is part of
Southeast Asia.

United States

The United States is the second-largest country in North America. Which country is the largest? (See page 6 if you do not know!) The United States is made up of 50 states. Alaska and Hawaii do not touch the other 48 states. Alaska is in the far north. Hawaii is a group of islands in the Pacific Ocean. The United States has many big cities. New York, Los Angeles, and Chicago are just three of these. The capital city is Washington, D.C. More than 305 million people live in the United States. They are known as "Americans."

The President of the United States lives and works in the White House.

The United States flag is known as the "Stars and Stripes."

V v V v V v V v V v V v V v V v V v V v V v V v V v

Volcanoes

Volcanoes are openings in the Earth's crust, where **lava** spills out. Lava is hot liquid rock. Volcanoes are like factories that make land because they have created more than three-quarters of Earth's land. There are volcanoes on every continent, but some areas were created entirely by volcanoes. Examples are Iceland, Hawaii, and many islands in Asia.

Lava creates new land as it flows into an ocean.

This Hawaiian island was created by a volcano.

Weather (e)Xtremes

A large storm surge destroys buildings, bridges, cars, and roads in its path.

Weather is made up of wind, rain or snow, and temperature. Storms with extremely high winds and a lot of rain or snow can be very dangerous! **Hurricanes** are powerful storms with very strong winds. They start over warm ocean waters. When the storm reaches land, the water becomes a **storm surge**, or a huge wave of rushing water. A storm surge causes deep floods. Hurricane winds destroy buildings, trees, and cars.

Other storms

Tornadoes are the most dangerous storms on Earth. They are funnels of spinning wind that move at fast speeds. **Blizzards** are winter storms with freezing temperatures and blowing snow. They make driving very dangerous because they cover roads and cars with ice and snow.

Blizzards blow snow. It is hard to see the road ahead during a blizzard!

Y y Z z Y y Z z Y y Z z Y y Z z Y y
Your Zones

Earth has different kinds of **zones**. A zone is an area with a special feature. Earth has different **climate** zones. Climate is the usual weather in an area. If you live in a place with winter, summer, spring, and fall, you live in a **temperate** climate zone. If you live near the equator, you are in a **torrid** climate zone, which is usually hot. Do you live near the North Pole or South Pole? If you do, you are in a **frigid** zone. Frigid zones have freezing-cold weather. People also live in flood zones, earthquake zones, and different time zones. For example, when it is six o'clock in New York, it is noon in Hawaii. What are your zones?

If you have winter and summer where you live, one of your zones is probably a temperate zone.

A a B b C c D d E e F f G g H h
Glossary

Note: Some boldfaced words are defined where they appear in the book.

archipelago A group of islands

coral reef A large underwater structure made up of tiny animals called coral polyps

country An area of land with borders and a government

equator An imaginary line around the middle of Earth

landform A shape of land on Earth

precipitation Any form of water, such as rain or snow, that falls to the Earth's surface

pressure The force of one thing pushing against another

rain forest A forest that receives over 80 inches (200 cm) of rain in a year

savanna A grassland that has a few trees and is in a hot or warm area of Earth

species A group of similar living things that can make babies with one another

temperate Describing temperatures that are neither too hot nor too cold

torrid Describing very hot temperatures

frigid Very cold in temperature

volcano An opening in the Earth's surface from which lava pours out

wetland An area of land that is covered with water for most or all of the year

Index

32

Printed in the U.S.A. - CG